A Good Cry

Also by Nikki Giovanni

Poetry

Chasing Utopia: A Hybrid

*Black Feeling, Black
    Talk / Black Judgement*

Re: Creation

My House

The Women and the Men

Cotton Candy on a Rainy Day

Those Who Ride the Night Winds

*The Selected Poems of
    Nikki Giovanni*

Love Poems

Blues: For All the Changes

*Quilting the Black-Eyed Pea:
    Poems and Not Quite Poems*

Acolytes

*The Collected Poetry of
    Nikki Giovanni*

Bicycles

Prose

*Gemini: An Extended
    Autobiographical Statement
    on My First Twenty-five
    Years of Being a Black Poet*

*A Dialogue: James Baldwin
    and Nikki Giovanni*

*A Poetic Equation: Conversations
    Between Nikki Giovanni
    and Margaret Walker*

Sacred Cows . . . and Other Edibles

Racism 101

Edited by Nikki Giovanni

Night Comes Softly: An Anthology of Black Female Voices

Appalachian Elders: A Warm Hearth Sampler

Grand Mothers: Poems, Reminiscences, and Short Stories About the Keepers of Our Traditions

Grand Fathers: Reminiscences, Poems, Recipes, and Photos of the Keepers of Our Traditions

Shimmy Shimmy Shimmy Like My Sister Kate: Looking at the Harlem Renaissance Through Poems

For Children

Spin a Soft Black Song

Vacation Time: Poems for Children

Knoxville, Tennessee

The Genie in the Jar

The Sun Is So Quiet

Ego-Tripping and Other Poems for Young People

The Grasshopper's Song: An Aesop's Fable Revisited

Rosa

Lincoln and Douglass: An American Friendship

Hip Hop Speaks to Children

A Good Cry

What We Learn From Tears and Laughter

NIKKI
GIOVANNI

wm

WILLIAM MORROW
An Imprint of HarperCollins*Publishers*

A GOOD CRY. Copyright © 2017 by Nikki Giovanni. All rights reserved. Printed in the United States of America. No part of this book may be used or reproduced in any manner whatsoever without written permission except in the case of brief quotations embodied in critical articles and reviews. For information, address HarperCollins Publishers, 195 Broadway, New York, NY 10007.

HarperCollins books may be purchased for educational, business, or sales promotional use. For information, please e-mail the Special Markets Department at SPsales@harpercollins.com.

FIRST EDITION

Designed by Leah Carlson-Stanisic

Illustration by VoodooDot/Shutterstock, Inc.

Library of Congress Cataloging-in-Publication Data has been applied for.

ISBN 978-0-06-239945-8
ISBN 978-0-06-283545-1 (Barnes & Noble signed edition)

17 18 19 20 21   LSC   10 9 8 7 6 5 4 3 2 1

For Ginney Fowler, who has put up with me all these years

Pat-pat wants to call you Gee-gee

CONTENTS

A Good Cry

HERITAGE
(for Walter Leonard)

The folk here
Are old
There are wheel
Chairs and people
Struggling
To push them

There are sad
eyed people looking
Up from beds they
Cannot stretch out
In

And some simply cannot
Move their heads

All will become something precious
Sapphires . . . Emeralds . . . Rubies which
Will be discovered
By other explorers who
Will polish and shape
The stones

And we will wear them
Never knowing
Whose loved one
We have
Embraced

BREAD

I was dreaming
I must have been
Asleep
There was a loaf
Of bread
Yeast not sweet
Crusty warm
Inside
I sliced a thick slice
Spreading unsalted butter
From crust to crust
All I needed was Parmesan cheese
To shake

The butter
Dripped
On my fingers
I was so happy
I laughed aloud
Almost waking
Myself
up

BEARS IN SPRING

They think
We don't understand

We are looking
From the woods
While they are driving
By

We tell our children
Not to run
In front
of
cars
and
trucks
and
buses

We need to tell
the cars
and
trucks
and
buses
Not to run
Into
Our children

BABY WEST

Baby West my godmother
Died
And left me $50 in
Her will

Where would I be
Without that $50

Mr. Gray who
Drove not taxi but private
Car asked the white man
He was taking
To the airport if he could
Let his "niece" ride
Up front

He also dropped me at
The train station
$10.50 for a ticket
to Knoxville

And a dollar for peppermint

I purchased a 45 RPM
But I don't remember
Which one

I spent the summer
With Grandmother
And Grandpapa

Not realizing a man
On a Latin schoolteacher's pension
And a woman who occasionally cooked
For white folk
Could hardly afford
Another mouth to feed
More hot water for baths
Electricity for the Radio WGN until it signed
Off at midnight

I had no idea
Grandmother had to beg
A white man to let me
Enroll in Austin High

Where I needed clothes
From Miller's and Rich's
Shoes, a coat and stuff
All I knew then
Was the sound
Of my father hitting
My mother every Saturday
Night until I heard
Her say "Gus, please
Don't hit me"
And I knew my choice:

Leave or kill him

Both were sad

I am in the hospital
Room
With yellow tulips
From Nancy and Diana
And a beautiful bouquet
From the English Department

I am trying to learn
How to cry

It's not that my life
Has been a lie
But that I repressed
My tears

We always teach
The youngsters

Don't cry it will be
All right

But crying cleanses

It will not be
All right

But we will learn
We can do nothing
About it

I have seizures because
I am thinking of my mother
Being hit by my father

It will not be
All Right

So I must learn
To cry

A POEM FOR JOANNE
(All the Time)

It's usually cold in winter . . . things rest . . . people go to the West Indies to bathe in the sun . . . the fish in my pond go deep and don't come back up until Spring

But Spring blooms everything . . . greens and reds . . . and lots of babies . . . I have to be very careful backing out of my garage not to hurt kittens or squirrels who have only recently been born

They all like the summer . . . and so do I . . . sitting on my deck grilling . . . having a glass of cheap champagne . . . listening to jazz that's as old as I am . . . smiling at the flowers

Then autumn sneaks up on us . . . I watch the trees wrap around themselves . . . the flowers fold back into the seeds . . . all the little animals find places to sleep for the coming winter

But I'm lucky . . . friendship doesn't have a season . . . Joanne is there smiling no matter what the weather . . . She is there wishing me well . . . no matter the season . . . friendship is all the time

I'm so glad she's always my friend

SPACE: OUR FRONTIER

We seek Antarctica because we no longer have Middle Passage available.

We seek Antarctica because we who are Appalachian understand the talking of the wind and the quiet of the Midnight Sun.

We seek Antarctica because poetry gave birth to Math and Science . . . not the other way around.

We seek Antarctica because the creation of America, despite the difficulties, is about Freedom and Adventure.

We the people are simply mammals upright. Just as the nation is having problems accepting choices of mates to legally wed, we will soon have a problem of what is legally a child. I have a son but I also have a girl dog. Question: Is this my daughter? Does my son have a sister?

Space, that final frontier, as *Star Trek* says, will pose questions that may not ever be answered but the one question Space does answer is: Is there another side of the sun? We know the moon has another side but we seek the quiet side of the sun. What life-form does it warm?

We seek Antarctica because Space is not alien and nothing is out there to kill us. We go on this adventure in friendship.

I think 10 or 12 writers from these Appalachian Hills, from this land that is difficult but not hostile, from these hills that stood for freedom ("We are not going to send our sons to die so that the Shenandoah can have slaves.") should go forth to seek our dreams.

I would want a 6:00 A.M. wake-up of the writers, myself included, get a cup of coffee, if they would like, and go immediately but not necessarily hurriedly, to our computers and share our dreams. We know that matter is neither created nor destroyed so there must be something that will talk to us in our dreams. We have sent photographers, engineers, other science folk to Antarctica. It's time for the writers to serve. It's time to bring an experience of the imagination to bear on the closest thing we have to Space.

The Morning Blog will belong to the Project; all else that is learned or dreamed belongs to the writer.

I would want an after evening meal get-together where we, the writers, share a glass of wine and our thoughts. Not speaking for any of the other writers, I would use my notes from the evening session to create a world for my readers.

NASA can rightfully say "Well, why should we spend resources on writers?" Because I believe we, the western nations, are going to privatize Space and only the well-heeled can dream of the stars. Yet it was the Appalachian dreamers who flew the airplanes and engineered the rockets who thought this a wonderful ladder we all should climb. We need our youngsters in America and especially the inner city and country hollers to dream of New Frontiers.

I see this as an Appalachian project since we are homogeneous. At some point NASA may have other needs but I see us as a group who are used to quiet, used to our own company, used to our dreams as the perfect beginning.

I see once again America leading as Planet Earth goes forward.

We need poetry. We need dreams. We need to offer to serve the future. We need the marriage of Appalachia and Antarctica for Space.

We do.

NIKKI GIOVANNI: A LOOK AT THE DEVELOPMENT
OF THIS SMALL BUSINESS

I'm a small business, I tried to explain to the interviewer.

When I was young my family lived at 1038 Burns Avenue in Wyoming, Ohio, a suburb of Cincinnati, in an apartment building. Aunt Lil and Uncle Rich lived across the hall. I really think my very first job was babysitting the Harris kids. I was always a night owl. There are probably reasons for that that I should explore at some point, but not here. Dr. Harris and his wife, whose name I can't remember, liked to dance. They had two boys. The Harris kids were too young to stay by themselves so when my parents and Dr. Harris and his wife went out to nightclub I was asked to stay with the boys. Or maybe my mother didn't want me home alone. It's strange how you think you understand why something happened then later you realize that you didn't. Anyway, this was during the era of 78 records and the Harrises had a great Nat King Cole collection. My favorite was "I Love You for Sentimental Reasons." There was and still is something about the softness of the rhythm that I love. I would sit in the library and play it over and over. I thought I stayed up all night but I clearly must not have. I'd wake up in the morning in my bed which meant I had been carried home. But I always made a couple of dollars. I have a sister, Gary, and she was three years older than I so I don't know why I worked and she didn't. Maybe she had friends or maybe she was visiting my father's relatives because we always visited my mother's relatives, Grandmother and Grandpapa, together so maybe Gary was in Columbus with Aunt Gladys and Uncle Bill. At any rate she always seemed to be home when it was time to go to the nickel-and-dime store to help me spend my money. I didn't have enough sense to mind.

Aunt Lil and Uncle Rich didn't have any children. In the morning they had a bit of breakfast then went off to work. Uncle Rich was a chauffeur and I really don't know what Aunt Lil did but they both left early. I know I was in school then because my after-school job was washing their breakfast dishes at twenty-five cents a day. I still don't know where Gary was but she was probably at home as it was school-time. I did the dishes, got paid $1.25 on Saturday and Gary would show up to help me find what I needed. Sometimes she would sell me one of her old sweaters that I had liked. I didn't realize that I was getting the short end. Which is probably just as well . . . I was happy.

My parents, like a lot of parents I imagine, fought. Maybe that's why I don't sleep well at night. It finally got to be more than I could handle. We had moved by then to our own home in Lincoln Heights so there were no neighbors close by to motivate my father to contain his rage. Gary had friends but I am not friendly so I listened on Friday nights and Saturday nights to the arguments and fights. No. I listened to my father curse and hit my mother. There was no balance. I needed to move. Which I did. To my grandparents'.

Grandmother, I know, knew the difficulties of my mother's marriage. When I asked if I could stay she said yes. Now I had to find a way to be useful. No one said that but I knew. I've always been compulsive. So I did the Spring cleaning when summer began; when I first moved to Grandmother's. I did a good job. Since I have always liked praise when she praised me I did the cupboard next. In Knoxville, Tennessee, at 400 Mulvaney Street we had an old-fashioned cupboard. I took all the cans and jars off the shelves and wiped and waxed the shelves. Then I moved everything off the floor and waxed that. In those days you purchased flour and sugar and things of that nature in big, big bags then transferred them to your tin cans. That meant there was always something on the floor to draw mice. So waxing made the mice less interested. Grandmother's friends who would come for Bridge, or Book Club, or Bible Study or any number of the clubs and associations Grandmother belonged to would always compliment her on how the shelves and things looked. She always gave me credit. So now I had a "recommendation" for jobs. Which I gladly took. And I didn't have to share with anyone.

It seems to me I've always been a small business. Now my business is poetry. I am CEO of a three-person company: Niktom. We have an attorney without whom I would be lost; we have an accountant because no matter how little you make you have to look out for Uncle Sam; and we have a scheduler. My scheduler is my lifeline. My mother used to say "If I want you to take me to the movies, I need to ask Ginney." And she was right. Ginney runs the whole show. We have at times hired other folk to help for this or that but my business is to write and my good people are there to let that happen. I am very lucky because Gloria was the first to come aboard. My mother and Gloria were friends and Mommy suggested I get help from Gloria when she, Gloria, opened her own law firm. Gloria was the one who told me I needed an accountant. Since I didn't know anything about accountants I asked her to find one. She recommended her own, Steve, who worked with me until his death from cancer a couple of years ago. Sandra and his wife now run the company. I found Ginney on my own. Or rather

Ginney found me. She recruited me to Virginia Tech where I am now a University Distinguished Professor.

If I had to take away any of it: the good, the sad, well . . . maybe just the reality, I can't imagine what it would be. Those early "jobs" let me know you don't need a lot of money; just enough to take care of your and your sister's needs. Ultimately I was able to get a fur coat for my mother since everyone else I knew had a mink. I didn't really want one for the longest time but that is another story. My mother should not be going to affairs where my work was being honored in a cloth coat when every other woman had a mink. I also paid off our second home and then bought Mommy a home here in Blacksburg. So I think money is a good idea and you certainly need some but chasing a dollar will make you crazy. I'm just me. Still happy. Still sane. Still a small business trying to continue doing good work.

A POEM FOR MORRIS

M is for Marvelous which he is
O is only that he's growing Old
R is that he's Really quite a fellow
R is that he's really Really great
I I'm not the only one who loves him
S is Simply everybody does

Put them all together they spell Morris whose laughter is
like sunshine from above

A HAIKU FOR MARS

When the man in the moon smiles
The men on Mars dance
To the shadows
Of lonely love
Of lonely lonely lonely
love

ASHLEY BRYAN

(On the Joyous Celebration of His Ninetieth Birthday)

One head
not too big

two eyes though
one will do . . .
but at least
one

two ears not necessarily
other than for balance

broad shoulders
we are after all
describing a man

two hands
two arms
surely only half needed
and with strong teeth
not even that

two legs
two feet
mostly for locomotion
but again
consider the options:
one mostly travels
in one's head

and of course a heart
a very big heart with two pockets
one to pump
and a side pocket to deposit
and dispense
love

don't forget a smile
and a hearty laugh
wrapped up
in a gentleness:

Ashley

IF I HAVE TO HOSPITAL

If I have to
Hospital
Please let it
Be in Appalachia
With the nasal voices
And soft smiles

Are the hospitals so
Efficiently run
Because of the Hatfields
And the McCoys
A lot of practice
Time

My arm is tattooed
By a nurse
Who can't find
My vein

I am here
Because I can't
Remember

A mild seizure
Like a little bit
In love
Brings palpitations

We don't know why

The medicine for love
Is sex
The medicine for seizure
Is _____

Somehow it doesn't
Seem to balance

Hospitals are like Grandmothers
How's my baby this morning
And they give you food
You don't want to eat
And needles that hurt

And you smile
Because you know
They know
You want to get well
Without
Somehow
Having to leave
them

LINCOLN HEIGHTS SITS

Lincoln Heights sits
On a Hill
Named for Abraham
Some buy houses
Some rent the Valley Homes

The Isley Brothers
Sing
Michael came to
Cincinnati to learn
Ronald's secrets
But He didn't have
The Mother to teach
The grace

Mrs. Isley moved
Her boys to Blue Ash
Where Vernon was run
Over by a car
But Rudolph, O'Kelly
And Ronald went
On to Reign as
The Kings of Rock 'n' Roll

Lincoln Heights
A little bit of the River City
Produced Carl Westmoreland
And almost one-third

Of the schoolteachers in
Cincinnati

The mighty mighty Isley
Brothers said:
You make Me want
To Shout

I picked up pop
Bottles from the street
For peppermint sticks

If Mommy had known
She would have been
appalled
What else
Really matters

EDUCATION EARLY ON

My favorite memory of my first years at Fisk is the Dining Hall waiting. We had to dress for dinner Monday through Friday. Saturday we could wear jeans to lunch and Sunday we only had lunch and a dinner bag. Monday through Friday was my favorite. We all would dress in, if not our finest, at least something very very nice. Stockings and heels. And we all went early not at all because we were hungry, or at least, I should speak for myself. I don't ever remember being "hungry," but the dinner line gave us a chance to look each other over. One of my favorite look-overs was Reginald Guice. He smoked a pipe which I thought was so cool. He seemed the epitome of sophistication and when I realized that I, an Early Entrant, had attracted the attention of Reggie, a junior, I was in Heaven. Of course, I lost 12 pounds my first semester because I generally gave my dinner to someone who seemed hungrier but I dated Reggie. I think I won.

VOLLEYBALL: A BALLET

(for #17)

Like a Fairy Queen's
Wand
The Starry tip in
The hands of the server
Strikes the ball

It flies
Over the net
Into the crossed
Wrists which bounce
It up
And over
And up and over
On tippy toes

Number 17 gently rolls
It over
To an empty spot
On the floor

Volleyball is not
A sport
It is a Ballet suite
We give points to
As we sway back and forth

It's a grace under
A lot of pressure
But there is no loss
In such a beautiful
Game

We give points for the same reason
The 5 o'clock Whistle
Blows

To count time

What a pleasure
To see Maroon
And Orange line
Up
To tippy the ball

Over to
An empty spot
On the floor
Go Hokies!!!

THERE IS A SCHOOL

There is a school
There
Which goes to the
8th grade
Where my father teaches
Math

I go to meet him once
Down the Hill
On my blue bike

He later said: "I screamed
'Who is that kid coming
Down that hill? He'll be killed'"

I wasn't but halfway
Down

The bike turned and
The rest of the way
Rode me
Down I lost Blood, Skin and
Tissue

It was the last time
I went to greet my
Father
There is a library
There

My books have gone
To Dillard
Where Marvalene Hughes
Is my friend

The donated Lincoln
Heights books are unsigned
Thirds
Marvalene has signed
Seconds

I keep signed First Editions
In case I need money
When I get
old

THE PAST . . . THE PRESENT . . . THE FUTURE

There is really nothing
We can do
About the Past
We cannot be unraped
We cannot or at least
Should not take back
Degrees because we no longer
Like the person

There can be no Justice
Only Revenge

We can't undo statues
Of Confederates who tried
To dissolve the United States
Because they didn't believe
All people are created equal

It came . . . after all . . . on a Midnight Clear
And we worship the Manger
Not the Cross
Though we should not fly
What the Losers fly . . . How
Dumb can we be

We cannot undo
The past
Not the people who kidnapped

Not the people who sold
Nor bought

Not the ships in which we languished
Nor the buses upon which we had to stand
While others took
Our seats until
One woman said No

We stand for the future
We embrace Peace
Not mongers for War

We cannot undo
The past we can build
The future

Where when we go
To Mars we send
A Black woman
Because she will make friends and sing a song
With them

When we go to Pluto
Which will be again
A planet
We send Black children
To learn to ski

When we decide
It is time
To thank the Deity

For our food . . . our shelter . . . our health
We will all . . . no matter which
Ideology . . . wrap our arms
Around each other
And be glad we live . . . at this time
On
This Earth

KONKO IN THE RAIN

(for and in debt to Kwame Alexander)

    the ceremony would have been canceled
were we
    outside in The States
but we
    were in Ghana
unafraid
    of the rain because rain is
water
    and water took us
away
    and water has brought us
back
    so the water that embraces
us
    that cleanses
us
    that quenches our thirst
for knowledge
and love
    baptizes
us now
    under Blue-Gray clouds
as we
    ceremoniously welcome
    Queen Mother Juanita

TOURE'S FEET

Toure's feet
Are beautiful
Perfect
He knows this
And shows them
Off in sandals

His mother I'm
Sure took him,
As did I my son,
For pedicures
Where he learned
To say "Thank you"

My friend has
Issues
She needs to keep
Her balance
Looks ahead
Not down
Balancing herself
Not seeing
The snail working
So hard to get to the other side

She steps on it

Ending its short life

I do not call attention after all
It is only a very little snail
Walking through a wide
Sidewalk
To a very big garden

I am sad but
I looked down
Said a prayer
And walked on
My friend had no
Idea

What she had done
To the little snail
Arguably if she had
Seen it she would
Have loved

And we understand feet
Delight
And destroy
They take
And they carry away

Anguilla Jollification
What a joy

THIRST

At 2:30 or maybe 3:00 A.M. I have tossed
And turned all I can:
I'm thirsty

But if I get up
To drink I'll have to
Get up again
To go to the bathroom

Thirst wins

Stumbling into my house
Shoes
I go to the kitchen
To find the lemonade

My mother
Were she still here
Would complain:
You don't drink enough water
Adam's Ale is the best thing
But I don't like water
I, like most Americans,
Take my water
With sugar and fruit juices
Or any other disguise I can find

Leaning over the sink
With a bit of real lemonade dripping down
My chin
I feel the coolness
Float into my lungs
And that blessed relief
That says Thirst
Has been satisfied

Feeling myself once again in bloom
I smile
Return to bed
And await my next
adventure

FOR RUBY DEE

I met Ruby and Ossie shortly after I published my first book in 1967. They were hosting a television show and requested the permission to use a poem of mine: "Nikki-Rosa." I was thrilled. My immediate answer was "Yes" and Ruby asked: "How much for the permission?" "Are you kidding?" I asked. "You mean I get paid to have Ossie and Ruby read a poem of mine on television?" And that was the beginning of a wonderful friendship. Ruby came to Virginia Tech about five years ago to celebrate *The 100 Best African American Poems (*but I Cheated)* with us. She and I together read the poem for Rosa Parks. I asked her agent what the billing would be. She said Ms. Dee would "Destroy me if I charged you." I loved Ruby for a lot of reasons but mostly because she remembered who she loved and who loved her. She will not be forgotten. Her genius, her kindness, her forward looking, her desire to build a better future will always be with us. Art is the right tool to build a future . . . and Ruby Dee showed us the way.

FISK: THE CLASS OF 1964

We came in the fall
On segregated buses and segregated trains
Very few on airplanes
Most by Mom and Dad
    To the historic campus
Of W. E. B. DuBois James Weldon Johnson John Hope
    Franklin

Inspired by The Jubilee Singers
Poeticized by Dr. Leslie M. Collins and the great
    Robert Hayden
Frenched into the legendary M. Jean Cottin
And maybe even jazzed by novelist/librarian
    Arna Bontemps's friend
Langston Hughes

We gathered
In the Chapel to pick officers and leaders
    We gathered
On the steps for the classic Class Photo
    We gathered
In the room for the photo of children of Fiskites

And some of us were grandchildren
(J. B. Watson Class of 1905)

We came
Despite what some Deans thought
    To Sit In To March To Protest
    To change the world We were living in
    To prove our mantle
    To ourselves
If no one else

    We were brave like Diane Nash and John Lewis
    We were foolish like some others
    We were challenging and challenged

    We were Fisk

    One hundred and two years after the beginning of
    The Civil War

    We were Early Entrants
    We were walk-ons
    We were transfers

    We were faculty kids

    We were Fisk

    Our legacy was not just
    The land that Fisk provided
    For Meharry Medical College and Pearl High

Our legacy was not just
Jubilee Hall which was earned
By the leadership of Ella Sheppard and those eight
Brave men and women who followed her to London

Our legacy is not only that the Queen asking
"Where do you come from?"
And hearing "Nashville, Ma'am" responded
"Why that must be a Musical City"

No.
Our legacy is that Fisk creatively conceived
Against the grain
Educating men and women
Together
In a classical education
We were not practical
We were not just job seekers
We stood for the ideal of excellence

We are Fisk

And we fulfill that legacy
by continuing to be
the Golden Sons and Daughters of the Future

Ever On The Altar

FATHERS
(for Jack)

Fathers are not supposed
To bury sons

It's not that the arms
Which used to hoist him
High
Can no longer lift

Nor that the laughter
Which he would emulate no longer
Comes

It's not even
That the tears
Bounce high cuddling
The Khaki cuffs

But rather that the heart
Which stops
And doesn't want to start
Again

Cramps the fingers
Which tousled his hair

And the eyes
Which reflected your pride
In him

The very idea of him
Not being there

Is not more than Fathers
Can bear

It's more
Than they want
To

BIG MAYBELLE

The room was dark
Dank actually
It was . . . after all . . . Newport, KY
Preserver of sin and soul

My boyfriend whom my parents
Trusted though Nate
Did not deserve their trust
Was taking me to a nightclub

George Ratterman would be sheriff
One day
And close Covington and Newport
Down
And Cincinnati would suffer

Cincinnati had gotten the clean money

The Living Room . . . Mark Murphy . . . Les McCann
The mighty Amanda Ambrose fresh from Chicago

Newport had the blues

And gambling
Though your biggest gamble was probably
With your life

I wore high heels then
And dresses just a bit above
My knees

I drank gin fizzes
Because, let's admit it,
That's not a drink

Nate said I have a Treat
So Mommy let me go

To a bar that was dark

Down dank steps

Where I coolly walked in
With one of the gamblers
Who knew everybody

We could see through to the back before
The performers came to the mic
The stage jiggled and CANDY
Was belted out
I CALL MY SUGAH CANDY
And there she was
Two tons of incredible womanhood
Balanced on stiletto heels
Wrapped in a black silk dress
Talking 'bout her
CANDY

And I who was born in Knoxville, Tennessee
Met one of Tennessee's greatest gifts to the world
The Girl from Chattanooga
Shake it, Baby
Shake it

This woman would never sell Girl Scout cookies
Or be seen collecting for Diabetes
She would never make calls for crippled children
    somewhere in Africa
Nor head up the Blood Drive
In her hometown . . . No . . .
She'd be leaning over the back fence
In a man's pair of house slippers
With a cigarette just sort of dangling
Between her lips laughing laughing laughing

Yes Ma'am

This was Big Maybelle

I stamped and clapped and shouted

Shake it, Sister Maybelle
Go on, Girl
Shake that thang

THE TASSEL'S WORTH THE HASSLE:
AN INTRODUCTION

Sometimes people confuse school with education. School is a good idea. It gives us a sense of community—we meet and greet people—make friends—get work done on time. Education is the exciting trip—the roller coaster our mind takes to find the frightening exciting.

Maya Angelou once pointed out there is a difference between "fact" and "truth." She was not the first to do so but each generation needs a reminder: There is a difference between education and school.

We eat our vegetables, meat and drink, if we are fortunate enough to live in a good area, clean water and good milk. We can do fast food and we can do fake food which will satisfy our hunger, though only very briefly, but neither is nutritious. We will get fat, obese even, and cause many problems because we turn our noses up at spinach and brussels sprouts or a slice of beef, you know? One reason you see so many obese people is not too much food and not enough exercise but fake food and a real fear of going out of doors to walk, run, explore. So let's explore this:

What if we hired retired citizens to cook grits, oatmeal, Ralston's and other hot cereals in the morning for school breakfast? What if the men and women who would normally be at home alone feeling useless were picked up and brought to school? The retired and the youngsters could have breakfast together. We could scatter the oldsters around the breakfast room taking care of the nutritional and social needs of both.

Lunch would be the same thing only we would serve beans five days a week: with corn bread, rolls, white bread, biscuits, milk, and maybe on Friday, as a treat, lemonade.

After school we'd offer a sandwich, chips, and maybe a piece of pound cake.

The results would be better-fed youngsters and oldsters who would be better-behaved youngsters and healthier oldsters. Now we have a recipe for education that the school can provide.

Maybe we need to recognize high school needs to end at the tenth grade. Send the kids on to Community Service; let them go abroad; give them an experience of service. Let them start college understanding college is a six-, not four-, year experience. Why six? So that the science kids can take a drama class, a literature class while the lit kids can do Physics for Poets or something without fear of ruining their GPA. In other words:

We need to change how we convey our dreams to the next generation. We need faith in them and we need to challenge them to have faith in themselves. Why not a class on the Constitution in the third grade? Why not a "Constitution Bee"? like a spelling bee that gives a prize like two weeks in Alaska? Why not a foreign language in the second grade that we follow through with until the second language is second nature. Practically everything we touch is Made in China—why not learn the language?

Timothy Wright Jr. offers us a wonderful view. *The Tassel Is Worth the Hassle*. He, too, sees the necessity of school and education. He, too, has a passion for the future. Join the sketches and paint yourself into his world. Have fun. Push yourself. Tassels are always worth the Hassle.

THE FLY ON THE WALL

I want to be
The fly on the wall

About to fall
Down
In your arms

I want to be
The wonderful spider
Who sat down beside her
Little Miss Muffet that is

I want to be
The girl you dream of
When your dreams
Float you away

I want to be
The fly on the wall
About to fall
About to fall
Down
In your arms

EPICURE

(for Joe who cooks)

Communion and sex
Are about the only things
That don't go well
With garlic
Maybe Mother's milk
But isn't it best
To introduce this
When they're young

Did I mention
Butter
On Butter I have to exclude sex
Because nothing could be better
Except maybe a long
Bone-in Rib Eye
That has soaked
In good talk
Or Kosher salt
Before being put
On something
Hot
To be ultimately
cooled

ON A SNOWY DAY
(for Morgan who braved the weather)

I like the snow
I'm a Tennessean by birth but mostly
A mountaineer . . . not from Memphis

I like the idea of something so light
It can gently fall on my tongue
Yet so dense that once fallen
Cannot easily be lifted

I am an old woman

So I enjoy watching the clouds open
And the beautiful snow fall down

I live in a place
Where sense finally came in
And schools and mail and stores
And all other things closed
Because it was going to snow

Winter Storm Warning

The signs all said
Though there were always a few people
Who didn't believe
And they went driving along

Until the trucks twisted into their cars
and forty or so vehicles on the turnpike were
busted into them
usually a few folk
were killed
some were injured
and the highway patrol said
if you want your car
please call

I stayed home

One student knew
I did Starbucks every day I could get out
She takes care of dogs and cats
And was needed

Morgan was one of the folk who
When they said Go Out Only If You Are Needed
Was needed
While out she stopped at Starbucks
To bring me a coffee

I didn't get her phone number
I don't e-mail
I have no way of saying Thank you
But more than Thank you
Thank you is when people do things
That could be done

The Coffee was way more than that
How do I embrace that caring
How do I return it
How lucky am I to have had
A student who cares

BLACK LIVES MATTER
(Not a Hashtag)

I'm not ashamed
of our history
because I know
there is more
to come

I'm not ashamed
of slavery
neither bought
nor sold
because I know
there is another
answer

I'm not ashamed
of dark or light
skin
straight or curly
or nappy—let's call it that—
hair

I'm not ashamed
of thick or thin
lips
nor that time
we waste singing
and dancing

we taught the white
folks
to sing and dance
too

I'm proud of Simon
Of Cyrene
Nobody made him
help Jesus
He did his part

I'm proud of the woman
who moaned on the ship
at the 10th Day
for admitting if not defeat
then certainly change

I'm proud of the Rappers
who Rap
and most especially
I'm proud
that
Black Lives Matter

We Do

We honestly
Do

STEP A LITTLE CLOSER

There was a man, Denmark Vesey, who gathered some of the enslaved men and women around and planned a rebellion. The irony is, had he been white, he would now be the name of a mall or there would be a great big statue of him for the pigeons to roost upon . . . but he was not. So he was considered a threat, a terrorist, something to be removed from the community. Being, rightfully, I'm proud to say, afraid of the enslaved, the planters were not content to be rid of Vesey and his followers, they also wanted to be rid of the means and methods of rebellion. They outlawed the drum.

In Africa there is a talking drum, much like the Native American smoke signals or the prairie dogs' squeals or mothers stifling cries in the night for their sons in jail or their daughters in trouble. There is a sound to let the community know something different is coming.

The planters were content that they had successfully put the rebellion down and by outlawing the drum they thought there would be no more disturbance. But the people, the enslaved, those without voices would not be quiet. The people used their feet for circle dance; used their fingers to snap; flipped their jaws with their baby fingers to set the beat; used their thigh muscles to "hambone." Every rhythm carried a meaning. Not like a telegraph or SOS. but like a feeling. Dance was itself good since it released tension. It also became part of courtship much like a good-looking actor gets the pretty girl each time. Stepping comes out of the tradition of competition and communication. Being watched all the time the enslaved had to be careful of their movements but move they continued to do. Some things meant things and some things did not. Like the quilts which led to freedom and the other quilts which simply kept us warm. Much has been lost or forgotten. But we still Step. And though we don't "hambone" much anymore almost everybody snaps his and her fingers and with the rise of rap the jaw pop is back not to mention the rhythmic breathing.

Cultures and cultural artifacts rise and fall as a people need to express themselves. This is good. "Hambone, Hambone where you been? 'Round the world and back again."

A POEM

(for Ethel Morgan Smith and Lucy)

sometimes the easiest thing to do
is forget to tell
those folks who mean the most
to you
that they do

I am guilty

I call when I need lifting
I call when I need advice
I call when I need to understand something

then I forget to say
thank you

chocolate isn't enough
and I wouldn't dream of jewelry

but a thank you
might at least show
my mother reared
a decent child

so this isn't even a good poem

but it is a friend trying to say
I want
to be a good
friend
since we are in
these mountains alone
writing what we can

and wishing each other
the very best

I MARRIED MY MOTHER

I know crying
Is a skill
I automatically wipe
My eyes even though I know
Crying
Is a skill

Maybe I will learn
My mother did
When she thought
I was asleep
I think my sister did
Sleep
But sleep is as difficult
To me as crying
I laugh easily
And I smile
And withhold any true
Feelings
Except once I fell in love
With my eighth grade teacher
And spent most of my life trying
To feel safe
Again
Though maybe I'm safe
Now

After almost thirty years
Which is as long
As I lived with my mother

Maybe that's not a poem
Maybe that's something else
Maybe I just wanted to show my father
That he needn't be
Cruel
Maybe I just enjoyed buying
The house he had to live in
Showing her she should have married
Me instead of him
Or maybe since we will all soon
Be gone
I should be happy I found
My mother in someone
Else who loves me

What else
Really matters

WE, TOO

I was home
In Lincoln Heights
Named for Abraham
As many other small black
Communities are

Only 20 years old
Not cowardly
I had picketed Rich's
Department Store in Knoxville
I sat in with Fisk University
In Nashville

But not all that Brave

Mommy didn't want
Me to go
Neither did my father and I wondered
Would it matter

50 years later I know
It did
We watched
We prayed
We, too, were
inspired

I didn't go
too
I stayed home
And reminded myself:
We also serve
Who sit
And Wait

WE MARCHED

(Celebrating the 100th Anniversary of the Founding of
the Sisterhood of Delta Sigma Theta Sorority)

We Marched
one hundred years ago into a sisterhood
We came together
in love and patience already called to assembly
by our mother sorority
We needed to . . . had to . . . must . . . break
Out
The Suffragettes did not want us
Offering only the back of the March
Our other did not understand us so we went
Our separate ways
But The Time Had Come
Black women would no longer Wait

We Marched

We Marched for the Vote
We Marched against lynching
We Marched about bombings and burnings
We Marched for Dimes
which the country took over
without giving us credit for the idea
We Marched for better housing
for the Pig Project in Mississippi
We founded the first Family Planning project in
Baton Rouge

Which was burned down
By bigots
    We recognized you cannot be antiabortion while
        supporting Capital Punishment
    By What Right Must I Birth Him That You Put Him in
        The Electric Chair
    Or in Prison for Life for a Crime He did not commit

    We Sisters of Delta Sigma Theta stood
in the Past
Dorothy Height was mentored by our Great Soror
    Mary McLeod Bethune
    Every President from FDR to LBJ had a Delta in his
        "Kitchen Cabinet"
Jeanne Noble famously boarded a New York train to put the
    Power of DST with Daisy Bates and the Little Rock
    Nine
    We stood for the Future
With Lillian Benbow to own our Satellite in the sky . . . to be
    the first Black Greek Organization to make a film with
    dignified images of us on-screen
    When there was a need for a Voice
Our Beloved Soror Barbara Jordan led the Defense
Of the United States Constitution and therefore the
Impeachment
Of a President

    We are great

    Our Sisterhood remains Strong and Committed

We grow stronger on the love we share

We Marched 100 years ago and
We will March 100 years from now because
We are Delta Sigma Theta
We stand for the Good and the Right

THE DIAMOND ANNIVERSARY

When we think
of American freedom we recall
the bang of trumpets to alert
"the British are Coming" and we recall
the colonial newspapers giving truth
to the populace that we must struggle
to be free as we move
two hundred years down
that lane we find African-American newspapers taking
on the same cry

those brave men
who rode the rails
the Pullman Porters carrying
The *Pittsburgh Courier*
The *Amsterdam News*
The *Chicago Defender* and our own
Roanoke Tribune
told the people of a better life
in the North
carried the atrocities of the South
to urge us on to fight
and sang a Praise Song
for our graduates and businessmen
our singers and musicians
our artists and dreamers

without the strength of our newspapers
we would not have known
the possibilities

Claudia Whitworth
is as much a hero as any
soldier on the line
as any front rider
on the bus
as any marcher in all the marches
for Freedom

it is with great pleasure
and much pride
that we congratulate her
on this Diamond Anniversary

RITA DOVE

(at Furious Flower 2014)

A raindrop
A snowflake
A little bit of sun

A smile
A tear
A lover's laughter

Some ancestor from
So far away
Whose dogged strength
Alone

Made the journey
Into freedom
On the strength
Of a song

What really is a poem:
Buttered Corn bread
A Pork chop browning
A Quilt being pieced
A Grandmother's tears

Or maybe
A desire
For a new world
And a Granddaughter to
. . . in the words of my Grandmother . . .
"Show Them"

Shall we call her Rita
And let's add an Eagle
No. a Dove
Both beauty and Ice

Shall we ask her to sing
Yes—Sing a Poem
For all of us

THE OLD MAN OF THE MOUNTAIN
(for Charles Steger)

In Autumn there is no question
Why they are called "The Smokies"
Clouds trickle away from the trees
As if the birds in awakening
Fluffed their beds

Or maybe the Old Man of the Mountain
After a good breakfast
Of grits and bacon and fresh-laid hen eggs
Lit his pipe

Some went scrambling along the floor:
The baby skunks, the mice, the squirrels, the little fawns
And even the fish
Start their day:
While possums and the others go off to sleep

I wish I were a Possum
But I have classes to teach

In Autumn the leaves fall
And turn
And ultimately trees will be bare
Awaiting the snows of winter

It's all so beautiful
And quiet
And we are a part of it
Because someone had vision

To see we must take
Care of ourselves
By our service
To others

Ut Prosim more
Gently defined
is:
That I may enhance your life
And so

We try

MORNING BREAKFAST ROUTINES

I'm afraid I cheat
at breakfast
and midnight snack

I always
keep salmon caviar
in the fridge
for morning
or night eggs

morning
eggs I sort of sauté
sunny-side up
in goat butter
and a side of grits
slices of whatever left
over meat is there
midnight with lightly
scrambled eggs
sometimes
if I have bread I will
lightly fry it
to have something with
which to sop

the only major difference
to me for breakfast
and midnight snack
is champagne
or red wine red of course
at midnight
to color
my dreams

POSEIDON HEARS HIS BABY BOY CRYING

It hurts, Daddy
That man who came
To play with me
He hurt

I didn't mean
For the men to go
They were fun
They crawled around
The sheep
And I found them
And laughed and laughed
But they broke
And they cried

I wanted to hold
Them
To see what they tasted
Like
Remember the Ginger
Bread men
Remember the Chocolate
Men
Why did the White
Men
Break

Then No-Man got mad
And hurt me
I can't see
Daddy
My head hurts a lot
Why did No-Man take
My eye
I only wanted to play
With him
Is he broken
Too

I'm sorry, Daddy
I'm sorry I can't
See
Make him give it back
Daddy
Make him give it back

NYC (Then & Now)

I remember a book store
Used to be here
    Walking down Fifth Avenue
In my bell-bottoms and Earth Shoes
    Smoking a cigarette
Because I didn't know the dangers
Of lung cancer nor the pleasures
Of wine
    There was a book store on this
Corner
    And that corner
And the in-between places
    I could explore
Life was difficult
    For a black girl
With no money
    Who only had a dream
Of talent measured by truth
    But passing those book stores
With a confident smoke
    There was the possibility
That's all
    The possibility

SURVEILLANCE

Who was there . . . who looked
Where was the camera
That Saturday night my father
Hit my mother so hard
She literally flew
Across the living room
And fell against the windowpane

Like a rag doll

Or a windup toy
That a child is tired of playing with

My sister has gone out
As she has friends . . . I suppose . . . and places
To Go

I watched
I watched over Mommy
I hear her say to him
Please don't hit me
But he does

She says to me
What goes on
In our house
Stays
In our house

I am a camera
I am the silent film

It was recorded because
I surveilled

I hid out
In my bedroom
With a flashlight ring
That let me read

Until it was time

Who saw what I heard
Who knows how to make sense of it

And we want to save the world?

What about my mother

I am a witness

I don't need an overseas enemy

I have a father . . .
And the band played on . . .

AUTUMN SOUP

(for President Timothy Sands)

1st you peel and quarter
a yellow onion (I know some folk like white
but I'm a country girl)

I like a whole garlic bulb
What's the difference between
2 or 3 little cloves and the whole
thing? Taste

These have to simmer

My father was a hunter
So we had squirrel deer
and possum
No—my father had friends who
Hunted
My father just talked so
They left him at camp
When they went out to capture
The protein

I am actually a better
Fisherman than Gus, my father,
Because I cast my line with
A smile and the fish are
Seduced

I prefer the red potatoes
The little ones

Though others like the white
And I throw in one sweet
Potato to add to flavor

Since we're not
Hunters I brown
The beef (with the bone
On)
Then peel and cut celery
Carrots turnips 1 small
Rutabaga

Now into the pot
And here is my secret:

Pumpkin Beer

It's Fall and Pumpkin Beer
Is available

Let it simmer
Until the Sands of Time
Go through
Or
If we were making
A President instead
Of an autumn soup
We engage
The Times of Sands

Either way—We're lucky

HOKIE STONE

(for Tom Tillar)

Some folk think
Hokie Stones are those things
Upon which our campus
Is built

I have been rocked as
The entire Shanks quad has
Watching Cadet bedrooms
Go up Though
We were rewarded
with
William "Add" Caldwell
Standing firm
Reminding us of our beginnings

Some folk probably believe
Hokie Stones curve around Burruss
Embracing the sadness
We have overcome while yet
We remember our fallen
Colleagues

Some folk maybe even understand
Hokie Stones are carried
From the ground and cemented
By workmen who risk
Their lives going up up up
To top our buildings off

But some of us know
And feel
That the true
Hokie Stones
Are the folk
such as
Tom Tillar
Charles Steger
Larry Hincker
And our beloved Frank Beamer
Who with their loyalty and vision
solidified us

Those with us Retired
Those with us in Spirit
And those in Hokie Heaven waiting
For new Stones
to be
yet
Quarried

INTRODUCTION FOR TIM O'BRIEN

Sometimes you see or hear something
That intrigues or disturbs you
And you go talk to that person
To see if you can help

Sometimes you are made aware of something
That you know you alone cannot change
So you contact your congressman write a letter to the
    Editor
Or maybe just get a stiff drink
And try to forget

Sometimes though you understand
You cannot make the tragedy go whole
You cannot make the hurt heal
You can do nothing but embrace
The best within yourself

And you

Write a novel a song a play a poem a short story

You can do no more than witness *The Things They
    Carried*
Your heart applauds *Going After Cacciato*
You remind yourself and others
If I Die in a Combat Zone these things
Are relevant

To you

You write because it is the honorable thing to do
You write because you seek the words to help all of us
    understand
You write
Because you are Tim O'Brien
And that is what you are supposed to do

Ladies and Gentlemen . . . it is my pleasure to present the
    incredible Tim O'Brien

LET'S CALL IT LOVE

If you cooked me
I would be a medium
Well steak streaked
with fat but not
Kobe

I would have been a contented
Cow
Obviously slaughtered
Before my time

When I was grazing
In the fields and country
Side I had made friends
With the prairie dogs the rabbits
The coyotes and wolves
Every now and then a hungry wolf
Might approach
Me but hungry wolves Approach
Everyone

One day I would be
Rounded up
And sent to my destiny
A plate on a flowery tablecloth

Flanked by a lovely glass of wine
And you
Smiling at me
With love
And pride

L.E.A.P. FOR BRIDGES
(for Donna Maria Smith)

Bridges over
Roads allow
Goats and baby
chickens
To cross without
Fear of being
run over

The steps to get
Up to the bridge
Are there for the old
Ladies with canes
In their right hands
And tomatoes in baskets
On their heads

Scarlett O'Hara holds
Up carrots protesting "Never Again" will I be
Hungry

But it was the Yams
Of the enslaved that saved
The enslavers
And those bridges
Will let us Cross Over

And the Yams will be pounded
And our spirits will be
Fed
And Peace will come
In the Morning

AFENI

(b. 22 January 1947–d. 2 May 2016)

When my lover leaves
our bed . . . it is colder
sometimes I turn
the blanket on and sometimes
I just get
up

I used to wait
until our dog jumped
up to sit at my feet
which gave me some
thing to cuddle with
but as the dog got older
and couldn't jump
I picked her up
though ultimately she decided to ascend
to Heaven to visit
with some of the other folk she loved

when the sun tucks in
the air is cooler
though it is only right
that night brings
the soothing warmth
that puts us to sleep

the same could be said
of Winter pushing
Autumn into Summer's embrace

Snow and ice will come
which is necessary for seeds
to grow
flowers to bloom
birds to nibble
so that eggs can hatch

but all change either
Right or Left
brings something cool
or certainly something missing

Afeni is not only
a cloud sheltering the sun
or the rain braising
the thirsty grass

She is also a season indicating change

She has ascended to the Heavens
to join those She loves
to bring the warmth to our souls
to help us
Grow

REMEMBERING MAYA

I must have met Doc, as we called her, way before I remember. I had moved to New York, Manhattan, to attend Columbia University's M.F.A Program and Doc lived in New York at that time or at least she was around a lot. We all went to each other's readings including the Chicago poets and the novelists who were around. But the first time she absolutely caught my attention was at Mount Holyoke College. Kay Graham was there, Doc, and others including me. It wasn't all that cold but Kaye and Maya had fur coats on. My mother, who was a big fan of the Seven Sisters, had accepted my invitation to come with me. We both had on cloth coats. Doc, as we all know was six feet or over; Kaye was tall, too. Mommy was four foot eleven and I am five foot two so we not only were shorter we felt smaller. I looked at that group and made a silent vow to never allow my mother to be with them again without a fur coat. We purchased one a week after we were at Mommy's home in Cincinnati.

When Mommy died I shared that story with Doc. She laughed. "We had no idea," she said. And laughed again. Mommy owes Doc.

Like everyone, I have read and reread *I Know Why the Caged Bird Sings*. And like that caged bird Maya sought an inner freedom. We have only to look at her life to see that she took every ounce of joy life had to offer. In all my years of knowing her I only heard her once speak ill of someone; and that was well deserved.

When Doc moved to Winston-Salem she was only a couple of hours from me so I got to see a lot of her. If I had any inkling Mrs.

Christ was frying chicken I'd go down and spend the night. Jay Z sent her a case of that wonderfully expensive champagne and those days I *had* to spend the night. I loved eating and drinking with Maya.

Everyone came to Doc's place which was great fun. You'd wake up in the morning not knowing who would be down to breakfast. The superstars; the wonderfully funny; old friends from another country; a congressman . . . you never knew who. And Doc treated them all the same.

I think what made her the force she is was that ability to speak to everyone in the same voice. Our mutual friend Alex Haley always said "Find the good and praise it." Maya took him to heart. She would always seek the good in any situation or she avoided the question.

Our only disagreements were about food. She is a great cook and I think of myself as a good one. We were arguing about Rack of Lamb which is one of my specialties. Actually my recipe comes from the late great country cook Edna Lewis. I went home after my visit and decided I should not just talk the talk but walk the walk.

I called my good friend Joanne Gabbin from Furious Flower Poetry Center at JMU to come with me to Doc's to cook. Jo is a great cook, too. We got on Doc's calendar, packed all our ingredients and spices and everything we needed and boogied on down. Doc sat at the head of the table where she could see everything going on in the kitchen. She inspected the Rack, checked the veggies and Jo was also making Blueberry Buckle. We set the table in the big dining room and dinner was served. Doc tasted everything and praised Joanne. I think she loved me a little bit because she, like my only living aunt, always felt free to make minor corrections. "I think the Lamb is a bit over-done," she offered. "Well Edna Lewis is in Heaven and I checked with her before I put this on the table," I responded. We both laughed. I know if the lamb was not done properly she would have eaten it and not said a word. I wanted to fry chicken for her but time just ran out.

This I know: Heaven has beer because my mother is a beer drinker and that's where she and my aunt Ann are. I think Heaven must also have great Scotch since I know Maya is on her journey, now.

A SINCERE APOLOGY

There are things, Maya, that I count on:

The sun warming
Bread rising
Rain refreshing

That the universe is fair
And loves me

There are things I respect:

My word to you
Your word to me
Our commitment to our art

There are things that make me sad:

that you would somehow think you had let me down
that you would ever think you had disappointed me
that you were upset with me

because you thought I did not keep my word to you

Friendships are forged with steely determination.

I have always admired you
And how you conducted your career

It is my Sheer Good Fortune
To get to know you and love you
For how you have conducted your life

This program brought us
Back together

I remember how kind you were
To my mother
How thoughtful you have been

I am so sorry I did not take control
Of what I knew would . . .

That I had hoped would . . .
Not happen

You were left alone

And had every right to feel
Not neglected
For you cannot have the adoration of three hundred
    people and be neglected
But abandoned
Someone knew what you had to hope:
That Toni was there

But you sat alone . . . waiting

I so deeply apologize for a stuck elevator
And a nervous cohostess who should have started
The Lifetime Achievement
The minute you got off your bus

And you should know
You must know
That of all the things I respect
And care for
And count on
Your good wishes for me
Are the bridge I cross
over babbling waters

You can never owe me an apology
Nor ever think that you need explain your actions to me

We are friends
And I count on that

After all:

I have bath salts to try
And some leftover
Johnnie Walker Blue

Have a good trip
But hurry home

REMEMBERING MAYA FOR *EBONY* MAGAZINE

Doc, as we called her, and I had a common friend: John Oliver Killens. John had agreed to come to Fisk University as our Writer in Residence my junior year and in visiting with him, his daughter, Barbara, and his wife after graduation at some point I met Maya. She was a part of the Harlem Writers Guild along with Rosa Guy and Louise Meriwether among others. We all seemed so much younger then.

Maya essentially, at least in our view, was a memoirist. She had already led an exciting and committed life and had many stories to tell. And told them so well.

I have always thought, after reading *Caged Bird,* that one of the reasons Doc was so good with languages is that she was silent for those five or six years allowing her heart and mind to absorb sounds in a different way. Much like Ray Charles's going blind allowed him to see differently.

Of course we saw each other over time but I think our friendship blossomed when she moved south. She lived only three hours from me in Winston-Salem—two and a half if there were no police around. The most fun thing was running down to grab a meal or a lovely glass of champagne with her. I could spend some nights allowing her housekeepers a night off. Doc was never alone as far as I could see. I'm not the best watcher but I did keep an ear out.

When Toni Morrison's son, Slade, died I drove down to ask Doc shouldn't we do something. She immediately agreed. We were going to have a celebration of Toni at Wake Forest, her home, but as the planning went forward Doc realized it was going to be more than she could take on. She asked if Virginia Tech would like to do it and we jumped at the opportunity.

Of course, anything you do with Doc will put her at the center. Joanne Gabbin was our cohost so we were in and out of Winston-Salem a lot. It was fun. Doc gets up in the morning, has a nice breakfast, chides folk like me about not eating then has a lovely glass of Chardonnay. I frequently joined her in the latter which was great. You never knew who would come down to breakfast, international stars, great choreographers, songwriters, politicians. You never knew. And it was fun.

When they make the movie *Doc: The Story of Maya Angelou* half the fun will be who appears at the table. And quite a table it was. I don't think anyone came into that house who wasn't offered something wonderful to eat. I once took a minibusload of students to Winston to see the Romare Bearden exhibit *Ulysses* since we were going to Greece later that year. Doc graciously invited us to stop by. I thought we'd just pop in and sing a couple of Christmas carols to her. But she had cakes and cookies and lemonade for us and, and that was a big *and*, invited us to her table while she told tales and sang to us. I had wanted to invite ten or twelve women to come to Doc's to record some Negro Spirituals this summer. We just couldn't get it done in time.

I certainly will miss her. Just as we were old and could start to slow down and gossip and laugh together she goes on up to Heaven to have a beer or so with my mother and aunt. My chances of Heaven are small but I will get a day pass to visit. Maybe she'll have saved me a glass of that great champagne Jay Z had sent her. That would be very thoughtful, if she does. And I'll take the fried chicken with caramelized onions and a dozen whole garlic cloves. And we'll all eat and laugh and get Merry Like Christmas.

AT TIMES LIKE THESE
(for Maya Angelou)

At times like these
We measure our words
Because we are
Measuring a life

A friend was not
Lost nor did she
Transition she
Died

We recognize a good
Life was led a
Generous heart
Ceases to beat
A hearty laugh will
No longer be
Heard

We measure not
The depth
But the width
Of compassion
And passion
And dreams

We place our love
Gently
On the flowers
That cover her
Under the clouds
That embrace her
Into the Earth
That owns her
And now
Reclaims her

We will miss her
Spirit Her demands
Her hopes for us
And therefore Herself

At times like these
We are sad

We gather
We comfort
Each other
Yet still
At times like these
We
Properly
Cry

SUMMER STORMS

The clouds
like my Grandmother
carry a load
they can no longer
support

Grandmother sang "Pass Me Not
O Gentle Savior"
The clouds though
crackle
their lightning and thunder

There are those who say
We should run
inside from the storm

But that would be
like leaving Grandmother
at the kitchen table
alone and sad

As she thinks
of her daughters

And it rains

EVEN AS A LITTLE GIRL

Even as a little girl
I loved to dust
Especially lightbulbs
In the bathroom
And polish everything
That was silver
Knives forks spoons
And all the little gee gads
Grandmother was so proud
Of

I enjoyed ironing too
Grandpa's undershorts had to be
Creased
And since sheets were all
Flat they could be folded
And ironed
Now the touch with electric
So they can't be smooth
(and you have to send them out
which can be too expensive)
but actually what I loved

was the iron that would scorch
the clothes
irons aren't that hot
anymore
feathers don't remove the dust
and mostly
I miss
My grandparents
Who took me in
When I was
lost

I PLAY FOOTBALL
(for Kevin Jones)

some people plant seeds
for corn and tomatoes and okra
which grow

some people clean land
and at evening you can see
deer eating flowers or just standing
Mother Deer watching her babies

some people live in crowded
cities
and they put out window boxes
with herbs
enchanting the folk who walk by

I play football

I have watched
men work too long
for too little
then come home
to smile at their wives
and children

I have watched
every Sunday

Sunday School children offer a psalm
preachers offer hope
a choir offers a voice
and join the community
in prayer
to a Merciful God
that life will be better

I play football

I listened to my parents
tell me to go forward
I listened to my teachers
tell me I can
I listened to the wind
whistling in my ear
and sometimes the rain
falling on my back
and I understood
the true heroes of our nation

I am doing my part
to be a part of
this community
this school
this team

I am humbled
to be considered for

The Hall of Fame
when I know the true heroes
are the men and women
who every day go forward

I play football

I hope I have done my share

.

THE MUSEUM (AT LAST)

President Obama wasn't there at
The Legacy Opening of the African-American Museum,
Maybe he like I would have preferred
Black
So that others would recognize
White
Maybe Brown
And always a combination
Though we don't always know why

Walking finally into
The Hall
Traversing through the airport
Security to show no
Bombs no guns no
Thing but our tears
And fears over all these years to get here

The Little Old Ladies
So dear to all of us
So courageous
So precious
Had taken all
The wheelchairs

They were dressed
To the nines
Their Sunday hats

Their makeup
Their high heels
Even if they couldn't
Walk
They were smiling
Even as they remembered
Selma and Nina singing
"Mississippi Goddam"
Even though they still felt
The pain of discovering
Emmett Till especially when their arms
Reached to embrace
Fannie Lou Hamer We Didn't Come for No
Two Seats
Understanding what would await her
When she crossed
The Mississippi border

The Viola Liuzzo who came
Because she couldn't not come looking
At the white men pulling up
To shoot her in the head
And they want to talk about
How they love white womanhood?
We have the photo but where
Is the wedding Ring wouldn't
That be a statement

Dr. Bunch was talking but could not
Be heard
He who talked to hundreds of thousands
Was not there to speak
Or eat how lovely
To have had Martin to
Bless
That table
The gentlemen in their Black
And White partaking of this table
Feasting on the beautiful food
And drink calling
Out to each other those
Who had survived
Smiling with each other
Those who had come
These 50 Years
Embracing each other not
On the loss of Martin
Or Rosa
Or Thurgood
But in the standing embrace
That all people are created Equal
And today we felt their singing
And dancing and drinking with us
Because today we are
For one
Brief moment
Free

NIKKI GIOVANNI, a poet, activist, mother, and professor, is a seven-time NAACP Image Award winner and the first recipient of the Rosa Parks Woman of Courage Award. She has been awarded the Langston Hughes Medal for Outstanding Poetry, among many other honors. The author of twenty-eight books and a Grammy nominee for *The Nikki Giovanni Poetry Collection*, she is the University Distinguished Professor of English at Virginia Tech in Blacksburg, Virginia.